Nine Hundred Moon Journey

Poems & Encounters
◆
Mary Lou McAuley

The Other Door Press

Copyright © 2017 by Mary Lou McAuley
All rights reserved

The Other Door Press
955 Clatsop Avenue
Astoria, OR 97103

Grateful acknowledgement is made to *The Upper Left Edge*, Cannon Beach, Oregon, for publication of "Susie" and "Amy Danger Waved Me Home."

Cover Image: "Moonlight and Poppies," oil on panel with silver leaf, by Robert Paulmenn

ISBN: 978-0-692-98179-5

For Robert

Contents

PART I	1
Gift Dream	2
Tissue of the Senses	3
Pulse	4
Companions	5
Memory	6
Lesson	7
The Salt of Doubt	8
Lost Rivers	9
Cave Painting	10
Anno Domini	11
Susie	12
Start	13
A Poem Is	14
Look!	15
Feathered Nautilus	16
Sue's Garden	17
Flotsam	18
Pat Metheny	19
Solo	20
A Heart Full of Yes	21
Just for Me	22
KSN 2011 D	23
Noctilius	24
Nocturne	25
Vigil	26
Drunk on Sunlight	27
Moonbeam	28
Superstition	29
Feeling Heat	30
Stillborn	31
It's Always Dark	32
I Am What I Eat	33

Feasting	34
Decorating	35
A Poet's Day at the Fair	36
Message from a Fly	38
Under Wraps	39
Sounds	40
A Prediction	41
Anagram: Listen – Silent	42
Bout	43
Storm Chasing	44
Hurry Isn't My Way	45
Inquiline	46
F-Sharp	47
Family	48
Land Ho	49
Cakes	50
Just Good Manners	51
Our Four Square Congregation	52
PART II	55
Paintbrush	56
User Name	57
Dreamer	58
Beneath	59
Messenger	60
Archetype Noir	61
The Question	63
The Visit	64
Clarity	65
Happy Hour	66
Umbilicus	67
Transported	68
For W.S. Merwin	69
The Weight of Small Mercies	70
In Circles	71

Not in the Obituary	72
Witness	73
Sharing Now	74
There's More	75
Death	76
Who	77
A-Musing Small Talk	78
The Archangel Bill	80
Killing Spell I	85
Fool's Gold	86
Can I Help	87
Note To Self	88
Stalking Horse	89
Killing Spell II	90
Ghost	91
Motion	92
Amy Danger Waved Me Home	93
Bus Stop Lullaby	94
Killing Spell III	95
Leaving Envy Behind	96
Siren	97
Remain Uncertain	98
Spirit Animal	99
Strands	100
Time and the Classmates of Sleep	101
The First Time	102
Wisdom Attends	103
Big Hole Montana Vision	107
P.S.	108

Part I

If I knew where poems came from, I'd go there.
—Michael Longley,
Irish Poet

Gift Dream

Years ago I had a dream
my days were a roil of uncertainty,
I was casting about
discarding
shouting for the invisible to appear.
One night, I dreamed I was in a forest
underbrush around me
thick and tangled,
and I was lost.
Then I stumbled into a clearing
where a junky old house trailer sat.
Inside a woman was banging pots and pans
in anger and frustration,
swatting at flies, up to her ankles in debris.
I fled, fell down, got up and ran and ran into the nearby trees.
The more I ran the more untangled the forest floor became
with sweeps of a clear way.
The trees seemed older with boughs higher from the ground.
In a sobbing exhaustion, I chose an ancient cedar tree
and sank down with my back against her wide body.
As soon as I sat, I heard a sigh
and the intake of a vast breath
then an old, old, creaky, sweet, young voice said to me:
"My roots rest on the bones of whales, but you are older than I."

Tissue of the Senses

The un-severed
phantom hand
that curled and held
the universe of sound and touch
the reminding twist in my middle
I once was floating
unborn

PULSE

Where has this come from?
Somewhere deeper or higher or farther than flesh
maybe all the way from the raging solar storms
now ringing the planet.
I am certain there are scientists
listening to the roaring.
Huddled, whispering, wondering
guessing the direction, the distance,
stunned in their scientific certainty
when suddenly they are only
recording static.

Companions

I walked along the river today
to remind myself of flow
of swell and slack
of nourishment at a cost
of bottom grit shift
and invisibility.
Obligingly distraction walked with me
pointing out discarded cans,
garbage cans' overflow,
gulls surrounding pigeon coats
filled with shimmering bones.
Daydream and expectation walked
cheerfully toward me
beckoning me forward.
There were other slow walkers on the path
looking down
scrolling their phones.
So distraction left me briefly
to trail behind them
looking over their shoulders.
No need to point out the empty cans
or the gulls.

Memory

Think of all the "I'll never forgets"
To him
To her
To yourself
that you have forgotten.
But that scent of deep tree shade
the pepper taste of low tide air
moonlight on boxcars,
these require no promise
that they be remembered.

LESSON

Notice the formation
of clouds
where there seems
to be nothing
vapor
realizing itself
expands in the
conditions of its elements
grows in height and depth
still vapor

The Salt of Doubt

Assignment: Write This Fifty Times: My True Passion Is

Desperate I followed a prompt.
You know one of those days
when you will only believe someone else?
Well, any other day this would have made
me smile but I was tense with wanting.
So, I got this written about five times
and I glimpsed
only glimpsed something:
the moment expanded
like speeding yeast
a sense of lightness in my back
a flowering along my arms and neck
I felt in my chest
that fizz.
Why I doubted the sensation
I don't know but the rising collapsed in that moment.
Too much salt kills the miracle of yeast,
too much doubt does the same
to the miracle of new words.

Lost Rivers

I read in a book that
London has twenty-seven lost rivers
I looked it up
the gist:
they are not really lost,
just out of sight
diverted mostly as
storm drains
stinking discharge,
hidden, unwanted
not flowing under the sky
in a river's way.
So by saying they are "not lost"
they can remain out of sight
a blind river without a voice
confined and told where to go
filled with debris, waste, death.
Imagine if all the lost, clogged,
rivers
could burst back
to a green bank-way
and spit out what we gave them
to remind us that
we, too, are not lost
just blind.

CAVE PAINTING

Above the roof of the house
across the street
a large, dark grey cloud
announces itself to be
a wild boar of the
Upper Paleolithic
it slowly dissipates
and as its rain presses out
a cave wall in France
seeps grey

ANNO DOMINI

Some things just get tossed out
I mean, I don't save a lot of things
that could and have had value,
but
why, oh, why would I think I would need a
resume from Anno Domini 2000?
But there was the form
so many lines and columns
Start: month, year, reason for leaving
Start: month, year, reason for leaving
I want to say: I've had a lot of jobs, lives, homes, friends.
I want to apply for this job
but
phrases like: "Leave no time unaccounted for,"
"omissions could be grounds for dismissal," irk me.
Maybe my impatience with this process
shows just how far away I have gone.
So, I just laughed,
and started filling out the form
thinking with relief
years from now no one will say
"leave no time unaccounted for"
the obituary will fill that in
for the bigger resume that begins:
Start: month, year, reason for leaving.

SUSIE

I knew him.
He had an old dog
named Susie.
Her hips were weak
so she wove down the sidewalk
with a flirtatious gait,
a soft, silky, big blonde girl.
They're both gone now.
There is a pile of old blankets,
plastic pails, black trash bags
in a heap on the curb.
Someone has been hired to haul
this home away;
each time they lift an armful,
golden dog hair
back lit by the sun
swirls away,
spins in tangles to the pavement
and disappears.

START

Take a black dot
and move it forward
press a little
up or down
lift your hand
and start again
this could be called writing
all the elements of movement
are there
also ink or lead.
So the hand and the black
dot conspire to lead you to a word,
well not just any word
but the word
not even the right word
but the word.
So have you guessed yet?
I'm not sure
but from my black dot and my black
ink, I'm pretty sure I see the word:
Start.

A Poem Is

The shared spirit
of voice
inside out
instant in the
marked page
my voice in
your hand.

Look!

There is risk in this step
this pace
there is a dangerous dance
in my mood and blood
reckless now and fully awake
it turns and curls
and is biting its way through me
opening me to reveal a tree in this night
that fondles only stars

Feathered Nautilus

There is an owl
in the deep water
of tall tree night
I've heard her
glimpsed her moonlit back
a feathered nautilus
she moves among
shadows and branches
so soundless in flight
I startle when she strikes
then the night closes
back around us all
no air bubbles on the
dark surface
only a star
and a watery smear of moon.

Sue's Garden

I haven't sat
in a country yard
in a long, long time.
Above me the afternoon sky
offers an I-Ching symbol
written in cloud.
Three short parallel lines,
pretty sure it means something;
nothing can be random in a sky
that is so intentionally sky.
I'll look up the lines
later
first I'll consult the robin
who reports on intention
and the lines that carry sky ink.

Flotsam

I'm pushing hard
to be ahead of it,
with my view of the river
plunging, dark,
new currents tossing trees.
The flood is coming home,
I feel it,
the exhilarating
race of water
and wind.
Others may put
tubes of sand
up against their doorways,
I hurry to be swept away.

PAT METHENY

Pat Metheny,
the sound track
of all road trips,
two lanes
overarched by
white bridges
each shadow
a full dark line
no greys.

Solo

I fill the pockets
of my ears
with dawn bird song
some songs I feel I know
some, I don't
but all day
I can recall
in vocal chords
I don't have
a song,
I don't know
but still sing.

A Heart Full of Yes

I have a heart full of yes
full of knowing how it feels
to walk straight into that
thrumming yes
those one after the other steps
that get wider and stronger until
they become a run of joy.
I have been there
and want to be again
to know without thinking
to know without asking
am I going the right way?
How false to think
I could know
without first setting out.
Sometimes a veil seems to wrap around me
and my vision dulls
so I drift, drift, drift
or,
do I?
Who knows. But one thing is certain
Today I have a heart full of yes's.

Just for Me

Slate colored, shimmering and moving
this early morning storm
waited for light
waited so I could see its veiled color
rising above a distant sweep
of falling rain
waited through the night
so I could find the right words
to describe dark daylight
dark clouds
because at night clouds are only
another shade
rain invisible
but I must be shown a color
so the storm waited for me.

KSN 2011 D

In 2011 the death of a red giant
its life force exhausted,
gave its explosion of light
to the Kepler telescope
for fourteen days
the death light traveled a billion
years to offer
all who could see
and understand
death is not darkness
it is
Light

NOCTILIUS

Rare, remote
I have only seen a picture
this almost impossible to see
formation
the sun's rays at the specific angle
so that a human could say
the conditions are perfect
flaring chilled at 250,000 feet
to sky beyond the unaided eye
who named you in this Latin phrase
"Light at the Edges"
surely the ancients couldn't see you
or was it something else they saw

NOCTURNE

Cupped in a sheen
of soft rhythmic rain
a neon cocktail glass shimmers,
truck tires on the highway,
a swish cymbal only a jazz cat can hear.
Every step in glistening
wet shoes
with tapping cadence,
a slide step slide
that finds the small scarved note,
the grace note
that always plays
above a city night.

Vigil

Yesterday we came home
and saw a small chickadee
had struck the window and lay motionless on the deck.
Only a few feet away
was another one just sitting there
I was certain it, too, had been injured
but at our approach it flew away.
I don't see this as coincidence, and
I can't really name it intention
so I held a brief moment of wondering
at the small word
Vigil.

DRUNK ON SUNLIGHT

Birds at the feeder
bright winged butterflies
on the nodding blackberry vines
and as I turned from the window
five tiny yellow finches
raced wavering
up into the maple tree
like the sparkling bubbles of champagne.

MOONBEAM

The moon
yellowed cradle of sunlight
pouring nutrients
calling life to stir,
to root, to bloom and die
each waking form drawn by darkness
surging blind
reaching for one memory alone.
Light.

SUPERSTITION

A broken mirror spilling light
reflections shading sharpness,
is that me
broken apart,
backwards?
Bad luck.

Feeling Heat

Turning my face away from
the glowing, muted television
flames from the fireplace behind me
flicker
reflected in my glasses,
rising yellow tongues,
just about out of sight
with a lick, a tickle of
hovering heat
like words,
just beyond my hearing or sight
laughter, and whispers
the stories of the non-consuming flames
the all consuming desires
combusting nothing
but surviving to repeat
a reflection only to me.

STILLBORN

I have been careless
distracted
what does that wonderful sentence
mean now
the one that zinged through me
when I wrote it
but then I left it there
like a newborn
unfed
un-warmed
oh, why don't I
ever begin to learn this:
write the gift out
it comes with food and
shoes and blankets
write the gift
all the way through
or you can't come back
and find a living thing

It's Always Dark

It's always dark
when you're a root
transcribing the message
of sunlight
the long slashes of wind
the punctuation of rain
you write in the darkness
when you're a root
passing the pages upward

I Am What I Eat

Another winter has passed,
another season of loss, gain
or the prickly in-between.
With the silvery light of Spring
my inner youth returns
ready for the fields
looking for the snap peas,
the asparagus
the green beans
and tomatoes.
I can leave the squash and pumpkin
to their winter fields,
another turn, another season,
and once more,
I can be Summer.

FEASTING

After a trip to the library,
our side tables
rich with paper,
thumbed pages shush,
the occasional thunk of one book traded for another.
We have pulled each one open like
exotic fruit
and like hungry creatures
looking for seeds
we sigh
or nod.
Pulling stiff paper
from a fan of
bookmarks
we choose
we lick our lips
we begin.

DECORATING

Oh, be careful butterfly
quick birds are building their nests
vines for drapery
grass tufts for carpet
your wings for a window
of stained glass

A Poet's Day at the Fair

Three Cups Coffee
I can't believe my luck!
Espresso machine and all ...

There are so many kinds of people for me to watch.
Two young boys are following their mother
through the flower exhibit.
They are holding hands to their heads,
not in wonder
but impatient exasperation.
Elephant Ears and Curly Fries
just paces away!
And still the dahlias and gladiolas –
an alphabet of flowers yet to go.
Their slow walking mother I can tell
is a scholar in the alphabet of flowers.
It will be some time before she reaches
"Zinnias."

Toward the end of the day
It is pretty much me
and the "Ultimate Grater" guy,
his company banner hangs below him
from two nails in a board.
Next to "The Ultimate Grater"
is the image of a large bandaid
overlaid with the red circle and straight line
No hint of a bloody knuckle, too lifelike, maybe.
One couple lingers, the woman wants to try it
but the man just rocks back and forth jingling the change
in his pocket.

A brief exchange and she declines to purchase a grater
but asked for her pieces of cheese.
It's nearly time to go
this barn is empty now,
except for the Poet
and the Ultimate Grater guy.

Message from a Fly

There is a way out.
But for this fly
the route is fraught with danger.
It is between the window and the screen.
On the other side of the screen
I can see the
shimmery lines of sturdy, well-tended web.
But, not far to the right,
well below the circle of silk,
there is a hole in the screen.
Have you ever tried to send a fly
a thought?
They get very jumpy,
at least my human-to-fly transmission
sent it into a tiny
fly-sized panic.
I have a small jar on my desk
it is for transport of spider, or ladybug.
All transport emergencies.
The fly is a new one
but the jar does not fail.
I released the fly from the porch
and was given a two second
'thank you' buzz.
I have resolved not to panic
when I hear the inner voice say
"there is a way out, right in front of you."
I'll also remember to say
thank you.

Under Wraps

What good is an angel in bubble wrap?
This one is about one inch tall,
wings at rest, hands against her robes,
a dusting of blue glitter on her wings.
I don't remember how I got her.
Probably in a package from Robert's mother,
sent to soothe us, bless us, let us know we were loved and
watched over.
I don't know.
I found her today
wrapped in a tiny square of bubble wrap, taped securely.
Well, Betty, I found our angel.
She is on my old square WestClock.
She looks both relaxed and ready.

SOUNDS

Sounds change their voices
with the seasons
a swinging gate in June
sings out the first notes
of summer
but in October
the boards crook their fingers
and warn that something is coming up
behind
you

A Prediction

See that dark cloud over there?
It has that look,
a look that tells me
it has begun to realize
its potential.
Within the softness
shot through the lighted edges
is growing a new pulse
and I am pretty sure
I am about to get a bath.

Anagram: Listen – Silent

Before I went into the house
I listened to the rain on leaves
bright points of sound, clear
almost separate
but in here back at my desk
there is no sound
looking out to the trees below
just the invisible stitch the hummingbirds trace
the dip of swaying branches
where the robins push off,
the arial maneuvers of swallows and the
arrow straight path of diving blue jays
here within walls, no sound, just silence

BOUT

This reminds me a bit of a boxing match
where all of us wait in our corner.
We have prepared for the bout
our hands wrapped
around pen or brush
shorts wiped free of ants.
Anxiously we wait for the bell
face our self
our opponent
and pray to stay
standing through the count of three.

Storm Chasing

Low clouds snagged and pulled
by a fast moving wind
take shapes of racing children.
They seem to be
hurrying to pull on boots,
forcing little arms into the sleeves of
jackets.
Hurry, hurry
toward that new storm,
fiercely needing to be
there for the first open-mouthed boom
of thunder.

Hurry Isn't My Way

Toward the end
of a really good book
I slow down
then in spite of myself
hurry to the end
it is like
heading toward the end of a full
and happy day
I slow down
relive it savor it
but also know it will end
maybe that's why
toward the end of our lives
hurry isn't our way

INQUILINE

There is a bee,
the cuckoo bumblebee
according to an article I read
they are specialized in that
they have lost the ability to collect pollen
or raise their young
there is no longer a worker class
just males and females
they are referred to as 'inquiline'
latin for lodger or tenant
their lease payment is death to their landlords
after feeding on flowers
a female will infiltrate a suitable host colony
kill or subdue the resident queen
sometimes by attack
sometimes by pheromones
the stunned subdued hosts will feed
her and her young
until it is time to invade again

F-Sharp

Our friend Frank met us
at one of our favorite spots for lunch
he had a achy, sore ear
and cupping his palm against his ear
said the echoing sound of
laughing, squealing children
conveys the note F-sharp.
He writes songs
music and lyrics.
I suddenly wanted to find a piano;
can Google sound that note?
Not that I doubted Frank
but I wanted to find out what
tone made my ears seem to
elongate and fold
and my teeth clench.
I checked Google with headphones
Frank is right.
F-Sharp.

FAMILY

The holly tree is going to be a grandmother.
A robin has been carrying into the prickly leaves
twigs and bundles of moss
when she has brought all of her furnishings in
she will press the moss against the twigs
with her beautiful red breast.
The holly will hear the first egg
cracking,
the peeps of first words.
Small toes will curl around her slimmest branch
new born, sheltered, warm, protected.
Other relatives will be arriving soon
and when the grandmother waves good bye
and she hangs her red berries,
the chipmunk feels its
time for a visit.

LAND HO

There is a robin
on the very top
of a pine tree,
it is leaning forward
like a masthead
sailing the wet sky
in search
of land
it calls out
is answered
and is gone.

CAKES

When friends are away
I watch over their cat
She's playful and frisky-young
snuggling her is my job
so I sit on the couch
and she jumps on what is
clearly her blanket
then twirls and rests
stomach up
then she curls and folds her
lush tail
over her eyes
but as I pet her today
I can only see her nose
what a lovely thing
just fur then to a triangle
of alive leather
the nose so rare
so ancient
of this creature asleep in the curve
of my arm
and I am arrested
purely smitten
by her nose

Just Good Manners

The rain fell last night
as though
it ran off the brim of a hat.
Just last night
the rain tipped its hat
and politely said good night.

Our Four Square Congregation

Our morning worship
supports a congregation of four.
As Robert and I find our
meditation places
our cats each choose a lap
Lily on mine, Woodrow on Robert's.
The prelude is their purring
felt in our knees as our breathing softens
and synchronizes.
If you believe some cartoons
cats believe they are gods, that we worship them.
But worship is a porous thing
so as we end our meditation with their purring in our throats,
they stretch and then curl
onto the cushions where we have been sitting.
Testifying that their one true god is the god of warm places.

Part II

The theme you play at the start of a number is the Territory.
The part that comes after is the Adventure.
　　　　　　　　　　　　–Miles Davis
　　　　　　　　　　　　　quoting Ornette Coleman

Paintbrush

As we drove from Seaview to Astoria today, through landscape very much like the fields and wetlands where I grew up in southwest Washington, I felt the stirring of a memory. A cherished memory of watching the Disney Storybook movies of my childhood.

In the opening sequence, a paintbrush moved across the screen. As the paint flowed off the brush, a full color scene appeared. When the scene was fully painted in, it came to life and started to move. I remember its moving tip bringing the color and movement of living blossoms to Johnny Appleseed's orchards, listening to him whistle while he planted the seeds. Its swipe across the buttes and towers of the Painted Desert dripping in reds and purples with smoke signals rising and 'tom-tom's' beating in the distance.

This is the memory that was seeping through the landscape I saw today. It seemed as though that paintbrush was still ahead of me, drawing rain soaked fall meadows, dark russet, dripping vines, the shiny blackness of my tall rubber boots. For some minutes, I was back once more on a childhood walk through fields near my home, filled with the belief that I was walking through my forever territory, my world as it would always be.

User Name

I was born backwards
and named late.
While my Mother and Grandmother
added and subtracted
reasons for my double first name
as well as a middle one,
my birth certificate
shows my name only
as Baby.
Who I am and where I am:
constant questions.

Dreamer

As a form of worship
my throat opens
not to sing
but to let the song in
the great inhale
the chambers lit up
accepting the swell of
pouring, molten sound
every voice is my voice
the quasar pulse
the signature line of this song
the wild geese offer it
the whale pod forms it
the wolf in hunt
scores it
the tiger's purr encloses it
I open my throat
to receive the voice
beneath all voices
While you slept, dreamer, did some sound
cause you to stir?

BENEATH

> *Everything real has foundations not seen by light....*
> –David Whyte

We seek enlightenment
pursue illumination
the brilliant light
but I have come to
think
we should be slipping to our knees
to ask to go beneath
far beneath
where darkness hides the invisible

Messenger

without meaning or sense
just the pulse
quick or slack
steady or faint
messenger – floor of the fire
I'll never see you, will I?
as you wrap around my shoulders
and sting the soles of my feet
messenger – floor of the fire
press closer
find a way through
I cannot aid your coming
nor prevent your going
messenger – floor of the fire
kindled from nothing
alone I wait for
your flame

Archetype Noir

Some say we are born with archetypes already attached;
the nutrient layer designed to feed and inform our ideas,
definitions and the paths we choose.
Do they come fully formed?
Or are they myths that travel time
to be handed out across the universe:
this for Anteres, for Pluto, Jupiter, Earth?
Here on our planet we gobble
up 'reasons' for everything
especially if a reason seems intended for our
species' divine specialness, so
I offer a short film noir trailer of Hubris and Nemesis.
The cast is always changing
the plot is always the same.
Now watch Nemesis, the best gum-shoe
in a low budget detective noir, tail Hubris.
We can see Hubris push its way
through the nobodys
snarling at the foreigners,
the filth.
But now, from the dark store front
a lone shadow detaches,
the street light is out completely or at least flickering.
Hubris doesn't really have a plan, just a need to be
somewhere more important, more necessary than
anyone else, even as the lengthening shadows of
cosmic night pursue.
Archetypes, if they don't know themselves
as only a theory,
will believe the story of
The One True Me.

The special example of why
surroundings and others do not matter.
"I am of my own making"
crows the surety of Hubris
propelling forward an unfounded pride.
But Nemesis, with softest tread,
has no need to hurry
ambush or intercept.
Nemesis knows a bit more of the neighborhood
has walked here before.
Reverse the spilled inkwell and you have the
dwelling place of Nemesis.
Always waiting for the first faint stink
of prejudice and judgment to reach a shadowed
section of street.
Nemesis is always alert and ready
for the predictable appearance of a new
dangerous fool.
Hubris isn't hapless
it has intention.
Nemesis isn't spiteful,
it has purpose

THE QUESTION

The young man
spoke from within the shadow
of his stutter.
He had a question
and after many pauses
his hands energetically
trying to encourage his throat
he placed his hand to his heart
and got to the question mark.

THE VISIT

In a moonless sky
a star seems to rest
on the eave
of the house across from us
I can see the outline of the
sloped roof
even the shingles
in sharp relief.
As the star shines
wobbling, precarious
I wonder
in that darkened home
does someone stir
does the cat raise its head
at the new weight
pressing down
this gift brought
by the new moon.

Clarity

I have learned that clarity can't be captured beforehand.
Only through the lens of the present does the experience become
    clear.
Like a steep stairway, dissolving, inky into the depths,
only taking each step will persuade you that all the stairs are
    there.
And the fear that snatched your breath
that held you tight was nothing real,
the steps were there all along.

Happy Hour

How many times
would I have
loved to have said
"Just keep them coming."
Sitting in dim light
a wooden table
sticky against my palm
while I threaded lime sections on swizzles,
toyed with folded straws.
But I never said it,
so, why suddenly do I have the urge
to say to the bartender
"Just keep them coming."

UMBILICUS

She ran.
She ran down the familiar sidewalk
clutching his letter.
Knowing she could never catch the train
still she ran.
Her feet swollen, her hands swollen, her belly swollen with me.
She ran.
There within the running woman's skin,
precise records of respiration,
blood pressure and the salt density of her tears
were encoded within the cells of my memory.
Stored in my tissues.
Physical. Present.
As I floated beneath her pounding heart,
another program streamed through the fragile membrane that
   bound us.
Unable to see the clenched fist against her heavy hard belly,
my new nerves raced with the panic from the pounding of
   her feet against cement squares,
my new lungs quivered and strained with her breath.
My new heart was imprinted forever with a phantom,
helpless heartache.
We ran.

Transported

Perched now
my window overlooking
the slant of yard
imagine I am a
marble rolling
rolling rolling
through the
blackberry hedges
to go ploik against
the house far below.
The CD playing is the one
I listened to on
the long drive back
from a workshop
and as a stormy rain
litters the window with
clear slipping drops
and forces leaves to
hug a slat of the deck,
I can really only see me
in the car
with the window down
speeding along,
gold-toned by the westering sun
and the clear slipping
drops of tears
trapping a strand of hair.
The music is the same.
I am not.

For W.S. Merwin

I heard you
your tread
your footsteps
coming up the stairs
while I sat thinking
of the images your
words showed to me
not sparing me
my great loss of
those big wings
that were there to
take me past the moon
to be the
great owl
that watches and endures

The Weight of Small Mercies

The weight of small mercies
I try to carry carefully
they are the moments of witness.
Sometimes tied to some kindness
also others
where I can only stand
and say to this world
"I saw."
These I carry most carefully
they are fishhooks in my heart,
their lines dragging
through rotting whale hearts
the white crossed hillsides of
clear cut forest
colorless piles of dead coral.
So I offer my witness
as a prayer.
And because I see
our entire beautiful planet
wrapped in strangling, abandoned nets,
I will not turn away.

In Circles

Once again
I have put my foot in the stirrup
of a circling horse
the reins in my hand
fisted against the saddle
pull too hard
and what I think I am guiding
is unable to move forward
simply because I think I know
where I want
to go.

NOT IN THE OBITUARY

Evangaline Irving was born in 1942.
Her mother, a kind, protective and very religious woman
worried after her daughter's birth
that it would be unwise to keep
the name Evangaline as the first name.
Fearing that Evangaline would be
shortened to Eve, a name that would surely betray its owner,
out of kindness she
renamed her daughter, Mary.

WITNESS

In a flicking strike
the man reached out
and caught the raised fist of the little boy
the large hand
encircling the pale and bony wrist
the child's fingers posed
for a playful punch
unexpressed
now the child's face
a frozen, failing grin
of the nearly born joke
and a quickly bruising hand print
shared
generation after generation

Sharing Now

A friend comes
who is a stranger also and
we feel we have met before
upon the Silk Road,
trudging the Trail of Tears,
falling together at a Freedom March.
We share without
a true remembrance
we share in tune
with now.
So a friend becomes
a stranger also
and we eat and embrace
and think we know
the stranger or the friend
because we are forever crossing the
phantom bridge of
Now.

There's More

His face, pinched by my kindness
after so much uncertainty
trying to convey
his "thank you"
his hair wet, his nose dripping
his reach with shaking hands
to take the two cigarettes
I handed to him
how stricken
his glance
when one fell
to the sidewalk's small puddle
"There's more," I said,
when I handed him another one
but I didn't mean smokes

Death

*Perhaps the Earth can teach us
as when everything seems dead
and later proves to be alive.*
       –Pablo Neruda

I used to think
that what was passed,
the past,
was gone,
over the edge of the world
dropped from sight
never to be seen again
but there is a curtain beyond
that edge
only those who stay
to wave good bye
see it.
We think the wave is farewell
but it is really a greeting.

Who

Who do we talk to
when the cause
the reason
we've left our
body and bones
is hate
or greed
or indifference?
Our only report
our only message
must be
nothing has changed.
The hearts are
empty
the oceans stinking, plastic-thick
the burdened sky stings
while little children
hold in their hands
flickering blue mirrors
to watch themselves
play.

A-Musing Small Talk

Do I know you? Sorry,
but I don't want to talk right now,
you know,
be interrupted
especially by someone
I don't know . . .
    Oh, we've met before . . .
I'm used to being quiet
when I'm thinking
especially in this café . . .
    . . . I remember what you said last time we talked . . .
So, no offense but
I'll just keep reading this new book
    . . . You said you wondered when you would be get back
    to the poem you had begun that morning.
Just this morning, I was walking
to the shop, looking for, Oh, just killing time
when I saw this book
in the bookstore window and it reminded me of something.
I almost went by but decided with a growing attraction to it
that I should buy it so I went in and . . .
    I told you when I left that I would remind you next time
    we met that you only stopped writing when you started
    window shopping . . . for other people's words . . .
Well, this is
a promising book.
    I'll look for you. Until next time . . .
It's about a woman in a café,
thinking, no hoping, she'll meet up with someone
she promised to meet, but, well, it has been a while

and most of it is her musing over all the possible
outcomes if that person reappears. I wonder now
why I thought it so interesting. It is pretty much avoiding,
killing time, with other people's words,
just small talk with herself, killing time.

The Archangel Bill

I had been needing a new geography. At least that is how I explained the trip to myself. In the evenings, I would sit for an hour or more on the front porch talking things over with my dog, Banjo. He could hardly have been defined simply as a dog; he was a four-footed radar unit, a gossipy, fussy aunt, and oh, so smart when it came to anything about me. The night before I left he was curled up at my feet, then stood to whiffle the night air. He had more variety to scent than I did; skunk, fox, raccoon, and the Great Other, that all dogs seem to recognize when meadows and roadways and forests dim to black night.

Moths began to thump the side of my head and flutter-walk up my arm or pause on my shoulder. There were two outside lights beneath the overhang and the longer I stayed there the furrier the air became around each globe. Banjo was trying to track a moth that had briefly lighted high on his chest, almost cross eyed, he looked like a drunk suddenly seeing something moving on his tie. Time to turn off the lights and go back in. We would be leaving in the morning.

Banjo and I spent our first night on the road at a tall butte in Eastern Oregon. Power Mountain the tribal elders had named it long ago. But its current name, Steptoe Butte, was named for the army captain who had obliterated them from the advantage of the butte's height. At the summit of the butte, I had turned the truck around, set the brake and put the heavy tool box beneath the rear tire. How close had I ever been to those familiar stars and constellations? Never as close as I was that night. I saw one shooting star and while I watched for another, I drifted into the restless sleep of a newly landed castaway.

I followed the Clearwater in Idaho, followed the Nez Pierce over Lolo Pass, camped along the Bitterroot and drove into Livingston, Montana, ready for a motel. I learned that many people were moving into that little town. It was developing into a haven for artists and writers. But for me it was an indifferent place, reflecting my own apathy at an empty destination I had thought would bring me inspiration and change. But this was not that country. Now, October was pushing September off the calendar and full on winter was coming quickly toward Montana. Each day I watched the snow line, with its ruler precision, angle farther down the distant mountains. There were passes there that I had crossed two weeks before, knowing I would be coming back. It was time to do just that. Time to go back.

Sleet was stinging my hands and my teeth were chattering as I finished loading my gear, closed the tail gate and secured the flap window. Banjo bounded into the truck, whining and wagging his tail. For two hours we headed directly into a dark storm. The truck shuddered in the gusts and the sky visible through the narrow canyon was blackish green, occasionally back lighted by the neon, eye-searing stabs of lightning.

The contrast of landscape is jarring when you come back into the straight, tan vastness of eastern Washington. Alone on the straight line of road I began to look for the old man with the donkey cart I had seen on my way east. I had considered stopping then, but I was going to Montana, full speed ahead. This time, when I stopped for gas I asked about the old man.

"That would be Bill. He has a circuit and we see him every couple of months." When I asked if he smoked or had a favorite snack, the gas station owner answered, "Camels and Camels." Back on the road, I began scanning both sides of the highway.

And, as though bidden by my thoughts, there he was, across the highway, headed in the opposite direction. When there is no traffic, some rules of the road seem to not have much meaning. I stopped mid-lane, drove over the median and parked a little way in front of his wagon. He stopped when he saw me park and was standing beside the cart patting his donkey. A small white dog sitting in the back of the cart barked as I walked toward them. The wind was cold and my cheeks were stinging.

"Hi. I, uh…" It had been so long since I put a sentence together that I was feeling tongue tied and a little uncertain.

"Oh, sure, I know." He looked beyond me to my truck. "Why don't you let your dog out. He's askin'."

And that's how it began. Raw wind howling at my back I trotted back to the truck, let Banjo out, grabbed another coat and his Camels. The dogs sniffed and trotted along the ditch a short way and then came loping back. They had done their dog thing and now wanted to know what we were up to.

He was working on a frayed cord developing a series of knots in the middle, but his eyes were on me. He extended his hand, not in a gesture to shake mine but to receive the gift that was in my pocket. Then he pulled out a plastic chair, inverted a five gallon bucket and gestured for me to sit down. As soon as we sat, the dogs had to squeeze in to lean against us; Banjo against my legs and the little white dog sitting on the man's feet.

"This here's Theodore," he said roughly patting the small dog's head, making its odd ears flap.

I said that Theodore was a nice name, thinking it a little formal for a definitely one syllable little mutt. The weathered skin around his eyes crinkled and he did one of those raised shoulder exaggerated chuckles from vaudeville. "Theodore is my name, and that way I can talk to myself!" This, I could tell was a well used story that had probably once gotten a hearty laugh.

"But at the market a few miles back, they said your name is Bill." I raised my eyebrows at his shrug.

"Names are only shoes, after all." He lit up and inhaled. "Thanks." With that simple word his voice lost the forced, jovial familiarity of his well-worn greeting. We both smoked in the lee of his little wagon. Nothing much to say. I relaxed and the land around us seemed less barren and empty. My loneliness, on its departure, had told me its name.

"Where you headed?"

"Back, back to my ho . . . where I came from."

"Inside or out?"

"Huh?"

"I said:" spoken slowly to the slow, "Where. Are. You. Going?"

Same answer, but I was sure I had heard another question. Although talking to myself had been routine on this trip, it now seemed to be a three way, and if what he said about Theodore was true, a four way conversation. I half expected Banjo to add his two cents as well. I told him I had been in Montana. "Helluva place," he said nodding to Theodore. And right there, on the side of the road, I told him why I had left and where I had been. I told him about the ghosts I felt on Lolo Pass, and the night of touching stars on the summit of the butte once known as Power Mountain.

The late morning had gotten warmer as the wind died down and we sat together with my blue plastic cooler propped open between us. He seemed to ask questions that were also statements about me and after a bit of this double dialogue my answers were less of what I had been telling myself and more of what I felt. My carefully crafted inner script was shredding, no longer needed, just as his comic Old Timer routine was easily dropping away.

"So, you just follow the highway?"

His yellowed teeth seemed to light up his leathery smile.

"Oh, sometimes. But mostly we go through and up and over and then we follow the stars and the moths, the bats and the owls." I looked at the highway, laid down in the tawny fur of dead grasses, the horizon was straight as a stair tread.

"How?"

"See, you'll never get where you're going if you know where you're going. Now, that's different than knowing where you want to go and where you want to be. Right?"

Well, I did sort of understand, but it was a heavier, more physical knowing, like knowing you had put your right foot in your left shoe. No, I didn't really see, but I liked the cadence of it and knew that by that very aspect, he had seeded some information deep inside me.

I left Bill/Theodore, Theodore and Lizzy some groceries and a bottle of beer. Turning the truck around, again going over the median, I watched my rear view mirror for as long as I could see them. Maybe he was going up and through and over into the hills I couldn't see, or maybe at the end of a long day he was just going back to a place where they knew him as Bill. A wanderer with the mind of the Cheshire Cat. They were finally out of sight but my thoughts stayed with them, my journey's doppelganger, navigating the flat empty stretches for me while I tried to make the climb out.

So I was back where I began. When our fears are ready to talk they can take on the aspect of common conversation; I began to wonder what had made them so potent, so powerful.

The house was dark. The porch lights were on, haloed by moths darting from eaves to lighted cylinder. I looked back toward the many lights in the neighborhood, false lights dimming the stars. And to honor all the nearby angels, I turned off the lights and went in.

Killing Spell I

I fear the killing spell
that has released its acid in some minds,
justifying slaughter
in a warped sense of
species rule.
All the birds
usually wildly singing
in the bushes and trees
are silent this morning.
Deny to me that they know
that hundreds of
nesting cormorants are
being slaughtered today
mere miles away.
Preservation's tame killer,
justifies savagery as necessity for what must be done
it seeks, against the universe, to take the fit
abandon the sick, the old, orphan the young,
hands not dripping with blood
instead they drip oil
to suffocate the nests
so that even other hunters
will die from ingesting the newly dead.
No wonder we stagger
to the end of our lives
forgetting everything
even who we are.
Millions of memory pieces,
our shared inheritance and shame
cast lots
to escape and be free of us.

Fool's Gold

Hinged and clacking
the skull speaks
with jointed arms
in fractured gesture
points to the gates
of the future
gold leaf has been
applied to seduce
even in the haze wrapped distance
a familiar tune fills the air
and we start to march
as uniformed men
form up behind us.
The puppet says
this is the way
this, now, is the only way
you'll be impressed
you'll be enriched.
My advice:
don't bring your sons or daughters
don't look behind you
tie your shoes and
Run.

CAN I HELP

A drop of water
from my toe
travels down the outside
of the tub.
So much in the news
has laid an unfamiliar
sadness against my chest
heavy, like a head laid for comfort.
After my shower
a drop of water
slid down the tub
like a tear on
the cheek of a stranger.

Note to Self

Can you be neither blessed
nor cursed?
Can you just be here?
If you think a god says
this is just for you
but not for them
you haven't
noticed the world.
We are part of a whole
that rends and dissolves, builds and collapses
and we want to see only what brings us happiness.
But wait and watch
see the collapse
see the dissolving
and you truly see the
life looking back at you
has been waiting for your glance.

Stalking Horse

Hunters of long ago
would walk beside their horses
into herds of deer or elk.
The hunted, who saw
no unusual gait
in the slow steps of the horse,
would return
to their grazing
until some were killed.
Then they moved on.
The hunters knew this always worked;
the hunted lived and died
without memory of the deception.

Killing Spell II

The tears began this morning
as the invisible string-pulling
revealed how much harm a puppet can do.
A grief of substance and dimension swelled,
unfamiliar to me, sought words of release,
a way to shape it into something that can lean
against the cardboard façade of hope;
because the sharpshooters have already been hired.
In your heart you know this.
Already they have numbers assigned like
#407, assigned to Management Sector 17.
What is now in the way?
The wild mustangs, the family wolf,
the soft footed cat,
even the high migrations that only sweep the sky?
There is a splintered, spell-bound ego that is greedy
insatiable, prowling, with a single red eye.
You see, the wild mustangs now threaten the
dead prairies, living grasses long gone, but acres for hire.
Now with all wilderness in the crosshairs,
with the warm ocean's salty tears already drying,
sharpshooter #407, to you I ask:
Before you pull the trigger,
will you fail to see the red dot
sweep across your pelted chest
before you realize that you have fired into a mirror?

Ghost

I'll lean against this the car while
you're getting married,
Brother.
Everyone is in there
sweaty, going to drunk,
but I'll lean on this car
smoke
listen to its radio.
They were all invited,
and the doors where you are
have been closed.
So, Brother,
I'll tell you where I live now:
it's a field
across town
trapped by sagging mesh fences
whispered at by vacant buildings.
You remember the place,
we rode our bikes there
and I died there.
Remember, Brother.
I can tell you the rest
while you're getting married
and I lean on this car.

MOTION

Tonight everyone
in here
is moving.
I can see it behind
their eyes,
their own private motion
except me.
Mine isn't stillness but
stopped-ness.
If they looked deeply
through my smiling glance
they would see it too
like seeing empty rooms
through
a glass floor
beneath their feet.

AMY DANGER WAVED ME HOME

Sometimes there are days
when you think you know
exactly what to expect
but then the day
you thought you had tamed
jumps the fence
hurries off to go visit the neighbor
and strands you when it
decides to take the train home.
Well, that's how it was for me one
rainy afternoon
derailed, irritated, pouty
"just want to get home"
my mantra
couple more stop signs
couple more left turns
then
at the next intersection
she's in her car
both arms waving
with a huge hugging grin
lighting up her windshield.
What I remember now about that day?
It was the day that ended perfectly when
Amy Danger waved me home.

Bus Stop Lullaby

I'm new to traveling our transit
and I am pretty sure the #10 is late
so I watch and listen.
Sitting here I have heard:
"I should have," "I was," "I shouldn't have,"
over five times.
This feels like a lyric with rocking lullaby potential.
Are we singing ourselves to sleep
with the past
as our present?
I should have
I was
I shouldn't have.

Killing Spell III

We learned from nature
to poke a stick into an anthill or termite nest
to lure the fish
to blow the call to summon the prey
but turn from the hunger we cause
the moisture we drain
the need for survival we've allowed only to ourselves
so we level the mountains, warm the rivers and keep
catching and catching and catching,
becoming angry that there are fewer and fewer and fewer,
fist to chest,
claiming it is ours alone.
Without pity we close our shops to watch an inflated, plastic Orca,
cheering for the terror it may cause in the hearts of our fellow creatures.
We shoot and shoot and shoot and with oil stop the throats
of parents feeding their young.
We learned from monkeys to poke a stick in an anthill.
We've come no farther than that.

Leaving Envy Behind

Today I sense I am passing
lives I have envied.
Look there!
The prizes,
the residencies, the awards.
Everything passing in a blur
because I see myself
reach for my own pen
my own notebook
and all I may have envied
passes from my sight
my ink now is all I have.

SIREN

Studied
to look casual
she tosses her hair
side to side
then the starlet sweep
like a comb over
silver crescent earrings
like gills glint
open and closed against
her neck.
Siren, mermaid,
mirror-practiced seduction
and we
who remember our youthful beauty
salute her
as she rises from her depth
to catch the eye
of a moment that is
already passing.

Remain Uncertain

You are uncertain.
I know,
not the 'know' of certainty
but the 'know' of a shared
kind of bewilderment
too many words on the loose
out of their pens
all expecting surety, promises
no, remain uncertain
I want it to be catching
I want to spread it
to kiss the one who steadfastly says of truth
I know
and blow my shared bewildered
stunned breath sighing into them
don't know
be uncertain
I spread it
I ask for more
and spread it

Spirit Animal

She isn't here but I feel she is here with me
ears back, looking forward.
Warmth held in a flank touched by a shaded sun, paw at chest,
curled the way our cats fold and extend a paw when purring –
 but also watching.
Gaze unfocused, ears relaxed,
watching in one direction, listening in another,
all within loose and supple skin, warmed and fired by sun and
 action.
How long did that moment last?
I hope this photograph was not taken outside a zoo cage
 or compound.
I hope a telephoto zoom lens stole not the big cat's soul, but
 its image, for just this moment
when I would look at her and hear her purr;
reach far enough in to see her rise,
stretch forward and back
shift her purpose toward what she has been listening for all along,
far away from the remote tick of a shutter,
she sees my shadow as she stands and stretches,
and knows I am on the the other side of the world.

STRANDS

We all have a beginning.
In quantum physics theory
we have many beginnings.
On one strand we may be here
and there at the same time.
Did I choose to
jump mid-strand?
Choosing this one time to reflect on
choosing this one time to chronicle
choosing this one time to say I was here
not there?
Well . . .
I was born on Groundhog's Day.
A day fated in our modern movie culture, to stand for repetition,
or to be associated with a small town rodent promoted by
   an enterprising newspaper editor in
Pennsylvania,
or back to an annual religious feast and even farther back to
   the pagan rituals of ancient Celts.
So, I have repeated, predicted and danced in a circle of fire
   under the full moon.
Maybe I have been everywhere at once, and this represents
   only one strand.
That way these pages can be true and false . . . forever.

TIME AND THE CLASSMATES OF SLEEP
> *Awaken; return to yourself. Now, no longer asleep, knowing they were only dreams, clear-headed again, treat everything around you as a dream.*
>
> –Marcus Aurelius,
> *Meditations*

Rumi tells us the breeze at dawn
has secrets to tell us
tells us not to go back to sleep.
Perhaps he is talking of our waking slumber;
when we sleep to conform
when we sleep to gain more.
Refugees sleep between shores
prisoners sleep between bars
workers sleep between shifts
lovers sleep between kisses.
Does the breeze at dawn say:
be yourself this day and
you have enough?
Do they say to the refugee:
you are already home,
to the prisoner,
you are already free?
To those who toil for pennies,
all riches are within you,
to the lovers,
your love is more than a kiss.
Awake or asleep
our lives are short
bracketed by time
we pass by,
minutes, hours, years.
So as long as I can, I will keep
listening to the breeze at dawn
listening for the secret that will keep me awake.

THE FIRST TIME

There was no language
no narrator
just the experience of being.
So as in a dream
I watch a soundless scene
slants of light
through dense
blue green wetness
the substance of sand
revealed as light flashing grains
not solid at all.
The thing I see swim down from above
I think must have been me
eons had just given me air and lungs
I hurried back up and away
through the swirling sand
then tossed about
learning to breathe
in the waterless world,
a world that started shaking around me
as I was lifted and carried away.
For the first time
I was going to die out of the water.

Wisdom Attends

In the beginning
symbols lie beneath the river's flow
whisper through forests
become patterns in the flight of birds
the horse's mane
the breeze contrarying the tiger's fur
the print of a deer
beneath the pad of a cougar
beneath the paw of the wolf
the tail brushed snow beneath the fox
the runes of the raven's claw.
These symbols are messages,
and when seen and realized
they announce
the waking death of another sister.
In her beginning the tasks handed down
were not of her choosing
but soon hardened into her choice.
Her cautious withholding
seemed like protection
but without the old instruction
she saw only the dangers,
the starvation around her.
Her body became artificial
shaped and described
by others for ready use.
If she did what she was told
she was honored
if she disobeyed she was
stacked in a field and burned.
So she scrubbed the floors

of the only house she knew,
fed the mouths open before her
opened her body to the damp smoke
of duty.
Then one day,
her feet sore and aching,
her center shriveled,
she walked out of the house
and knelt at a stream.
She was joined by an old woman
who sat beside her and began
to rub her feet.
But she was not a silent attendant.
She sang and cooed as she rubbed.
And then was gone.
When she stood once again,
slivers of thought, pin holes in her vision appeared
as though a thread had been pulled in her awareness of the world.
And the other voice
a reasonable, assured, dismissive voice
began to fade.
It was the voice of our culture;
taming, always taming the thoughts,
banking the fires of abundance,
always saving what was sure to run out
the life force must wane,
not everything you want is possible,
it is too good to be true,
rules are to protect you,
attract attention and you will be ridiculous.
When she returned to her house
after so long away
it seemed small, alien

all the images of her occupation
were distortions, dissolving.
She crossed her threshold
and around her
heard the murmured singing
of her wise sisters.
Their chanting was for her old life;
it was a death chant.
For some time
she raged in regret
for what she hadn't known,
hadn't done,
hadn't realized,
hadn't remembered.
Raged that no one told her
that all of her caution was pointless
that all she'd given was emptiness.
For some time she raged in defiance
of what seemed unfair,
she'd always done
what she was told.
For sometime she raged in
a sort of happy anger
at the old women
who were visiting her dreams.
Wisdom endures
she is the handmaiden of death and change,
transferring death's
gentleness to those who fear
the fairy tale monsters of this world.
Death in her glorious joy
has been wrapped in a stunning
spell of darkness and smoke

to appear as a red-eyed, cragged,
grasping, towering male.
So wisdom rubs the feet
and sings to all who feel their changing as a fearsome death
and seeds the world with symbols
always pulling at the masking spell.
The spell can be broken
this wisdom knows.

Big Hole Montana Vision

Staring at the road, squinting against the glare of a dusty sun, on the inner screen of some memory and mind I watched the other woman run. And I knew at once, the running ghost was old. Her movements were far from swift but were like the trot of a resolute dog, the kind of motion that once learned can keep you going for miles and hours. This was not a panicked sprint. She would not be stopped, she would not fall to the side. She was already a spirit heading home. You will not take me, I have died to that life. Maybe there were shouts behind her, perhaps a warning shot. Probably just joking agreement that one less old woman on the trail was going to make the job easier; not worth a bullet. Were there dark eyes watching her back, did they spark for a moment before they returned to their own shuffling feet?

Before I got back in the truck, I had to wait for my breath to return to normal, as if I had been running too.

P.S.

When you find you can go neither backward nor forward, when you discover that you are no longer able to stand, sit or lie down, when your children have died of malnutrition and your aged parents have been sent to the poorhouse or the gas chamber, when you realize that you can neither write nor not write, when you are convinced that all the exits are blocked, either you take to believing in miracles or you stand still like the hummingbird. The miracle is that the honey is always there, right under your nose, only you were too busy searching elsewhere to realize it. The worst is not death but being blind, blind to the fact that everything about life is in the nature of the miraculous.

–Henry Miller
Stand Still Like The Hummingbird,
1962

ACKNOWLEDGEMENTS

Christi Payne, Page & Book, designed and formatted this book. Her guidance, support and dedication to my work has brought it to you.

Finally, a thank you to all I have encountered on this journey; the Territory and the Adventure.

Cover Image: 'Moonlight and Poppies,' oil on panel with silver leaf, by Robert Paulmenn

www.ingramcontent.com/pod-product-compliance
Lightning Source LLC
Chambersburg PA
CBHW031425290426
44110CB00011B/525